THE SWEET SUCKER PUNCH

REVISED EDITION

THE SWEET SUCKER PUNCH

REVISED EDITION

Written By
Xavier "Bad Pads" Biggs

Edited by
DJ Nabs
Elliot Lloyd
Cynthia Biggs El

Cover Art by
Elliot Lloyd

ISBN-13: 978-1492921271

ISBN-10: 1492921270

Dedication

The Sweet Sucker Punch, my first memoir, is dedicated to the memory of my beautiful mother, Mary Jeanette Biggs. Your strong, sweet spirit will live forever in bliss in heaven. We miss you, mom, and love you dearly. You are always in our thoughts. We will continue to soldier towards righteousness and good in honor of your name.

A Champion's Poem

By Xavier Biggs

Stick and Move the Adversity
Bob and Weave the Negativity
Attack Obstacles with a Left-Right Combination
To Increase Your Title Shot Qualifications
To Become Champion of Life

Xavier "Bad Pads" Biggs

Table of Contents

Xavier Biggs

Introduction

by Tyrell Biggs

Reflecting on all my accomplishments and adventures in the world of boxing, I can truly say that I am blessed. Although it was definitely a journey of great highs and major lows, every experience, whether good or bad, was enlightening and stimulating. I've met and hung out with movie stars, entertainers, famous athletes, and even shook hands with presidents.

Boxing is an extremely challenging and unforgiving sport. Very few make it to world-class status, and that's why I feel so fortunate and blessed. Now that my boxing career is over, my whole perspective on life has drastically changed. Boxing allowed me to view life in ways that most men could only imagine. In the end, my greatest reward was enduring it with all my faculties intact; and, hopefully, I can provide positive inspiration and hope for those in need.

Since I caught the world's attention by becoming the first ever Olympic Super Heavyweight champion -- amateur boxing's most valued and prestigious title — I pursued a world-class professional boxing career, competing against some of the best heavyweights of the era, such as Mike Tyson, Riddick Bowe, Lennox Lewis, James "Quick" Tillis, Angel Milan, Mitch Green, Tony Tubbs, Larry Donald, Renaldo Snipes and David Bey. I even had a ten-rounder with the slick, beefed-up-to-heavyweight-from-cruiserweight Puerto Rican Ossie Occasio. I won some and lost some. But every fight provided a significant learning experience.

Now, as I sit in Philly, I reflect on all my accomplishments, realizing that they were all for a divine purpose. Although I had a spectacular professional career and won every amateur title on the books, I made some bad mistakes — and had to deal with the consequences. But I thank God for my experiences during my boxing years because they played an important part in helping me endure the adversities, especially the enormous challenge of crack and alcohol addiction. I slipped into it easily at such a young age due to all that early success. But because of the discipline and will that I had mustered up for boxing, I transferred the same determination towards achieving 27 years of sobriety — never relapsing, not even once. Now I strive to be an example for anyone suffering the misfortune of committing mistakes that I made.

I remember the awesome, gratifying feeling after visiting young cancer patients. About a month after my visit, I checked on the children, and the doctors informed me that their conditions improved after viewing the tape from my Olympic gold medal win. I knew then that, despite all I'd experienced – good and bad – it was all worthwhile. My experiences are a source of positive enlightenment to others, and that's why I'm supporting my brother, Xavier, in writing these exhilarating, inspiring short stories of his own boxing experiences. I am totally convinced that this is God's work, and this is my mission.

Foreword

by Xavier Biggs

Most of the boxing stories I read have a negative twist. Although boxing does have its dark side, it offers lots of positive effects. There's more to boxing than just training and conditioning someone to get in a square ring and pulverize someone else. Although defeating an opponent is boxing's intent, aspects of its training, preparation and overall culture generally apply to life and character building. Boxing instills a sense of honor, bravery, discipline, mental and physical conditioning and integrity. Boxing is an art. Its movement encompasses style and grace, and intellect is displayed in the brilliance of strategy. These elements are also essential when one seeks to pursue success in life. I had a very short — but undefeated — amateur career followed by a shorter professional career (4 wins, 4 losses and 2 draws). My career, spread out over seven years in Philly's heavily cultured boxing scene, came without a promoter. I then graduated to boxing's elite level when I retired from fighting to accompany my brother Tyrell, as his assistant. We traveled around the world attending world-class training camps and promotions.

That school of boxing was a Harvard-type learning experience. My losses were at once humbling and rectitudinous; the wins were extraordinary self-esteem strengtheners. All of this applies to everyday life, which explains my motive for writing these short stories. I seek to reel the reader into the fascinating and stimulating world of true boxing by acknowledging the positive benefits this unique sport can provide, despite its tempestuous, violent nature.

Since I moved to Atlanta in 1988, I've run five boxing gyms, dabbled in some promotions and established a thriving fitness program using boxing training concepts. A few of my students went on to launch life-altering fitness programs and promotions, affording great mental and physical benefits for people from all walks of life.

One of my students, a female boxer who is a Guinness Book of World Records world champion, now promotes a corporate boxing charity in which contestants "put it all on the line", duking it out for causes dear to their heart. Another one of my students, currently a world kickboxing champion, started a rapidly growing boxing and kickboxing fitness franchise inspired by our concept. These programs are changing the lives of everyday people. Hopefully, these short boxing stories will reinforce boxing's benefits.

George Benton

Chapter 1: A Tribute to Georgie Benton (1933-2011)

It was a balmy spring day in Philly and I was feeling battle ready, so I decided to cruise North Philly and visit “Smoking” Joe Frazier’s Cloverlay Gym on Broad Street. I needed unfamiliar sparring to keep my guns sharp. It was about 1 p.m., a slow time at the gym. There were only a few boxers and a couple of trainers milling around. I remember it well, that nostril-attacking odor of sweaty gloves and pungent hand-wraps when opening the door. But this smell was spiked with the hint of a familiar, exotically sweet aroma. It was Georgie Benton's cologne wafting the stale air as he strutted around the floor in his tailor-made outfit and big-brimmed hat angled on his head. Then, that unmistakably raspy voice: "AAYY, Baby Cakes, what's happ'nin'?"

Ol' Georgie, as he was known, leaned against the wall, a Daily News under his arm – a real 'slickster'. I was glad to see him and replied, "Hey, Georgie. Wassup? Anybody around I can get some rounds in with?" Right then, some dude came busting through the door with an entourage of about nine or 10 teenage kids, all yapping his praises. He paraded across the gym to the locker room, his fan club tagging behind.

Georgie looked up and said, "There's your ring work right there." I said, "OK, cool, but who's that?" Georgie just nonchalantly responded, "Ah, just some showoff kid that ain't going nowhere." He wasn't impressed. But I was curious: "Yeah, but can he fight?" He pointed his squinty eyes in my direction: "Just good enough to keep you honest." "Good," I said. "That's what I need."

When I returned, dressed and ready, the showoff cat was already on the gym floor stretching, his adolescent cheerleaders standing around, verbally expressing their admiration. It was obvious he wasn't just there to train. He wanted to put on a show. His silver boxing shoes sparkled, laden with gaudy tassels, and were complemented by silver-and-black velvet trunks. His body was heavily greased with Vaseline to give his muscles extra glean. I felt kind of corny in my heather gray sweatshirt and sweatpants. Catching his eye, he sized me up. That's when I knew Georgie had asked him about sparring – when he sized me up. That's when I knew Georgie had asked him about sparring – when I was in the locker room. We just acknowledged each other and gave a fist-tap greeting before warming up.

I noticed his fan club curiously studying me shadowbox. I might've been caught up in the hype, as I was outclassed and outmaneuvered for the first two rounds. He wasn't fast but had unfamiliar moves. When the bell rang ending the second round, I was embarrassed. "Yo, Georgie! What do I do with this guy?" I pleaded. Georgie seemed a little fed up, too: "Listen man, when I say 'Go!' just shoot the right hand at him." I was puzzled: "That's it?" He impatiently snapped back, "Don't think; don't hesitate. As soon as you hear me say 'Go!' shoot it fast, a straight right-hand – right down the pike. You hear me?" I shrugged my shoulders: "Ok."

Although I was a little perplexed, deep down, I knew Georgie had seen something. When the bell rang for the third round, I went in behind a busy jab, anticipating

Georgie's signal. Meanwhile, my sparring partner danced around the ring, entertaining his young, impressionable followers with a little creative posturing. About a minute into the round, I finally heard that raspy voice: "Go!" My right hand was already cocked and ready. Georgie was the trigger releasing the torpedo. It came fast with no warning, like brown-skinned lightning. It made solid impact. I don't know exactly where, but definitely around the head and shoulder area. The dude went down hard and fast. I heard some trainer across the gym yelp in amazement. Georgie just half-smiled and nodded in satisfaction.

My sparring partner pulled himself up from off the canvas, wide-eyed, dazed and humiliated. His admiring attendants were silent; their mouths wide open. I felt kind of sorry for him, and the next round I just transferred my attack to the body and feinted headshots, just keeping him on defense.

After the session, Georgie had very few words. "You are better than you think you are. Now go over and work the bag a few rounds, power combinations with dead weight," he said. "I gotta lunch date with some cute fox I met yesterday. See ya later." He turned and strolled out the gym with a swagger very few men could emulate.

Georgie was an old slickster with a gigantic presence and original style. He was truly one of the master teachers of the 'sweet science'. He was assistant trainer to the great Eddie Futch, and in Joe Frazier's corner against Muhammad Ali for "The Thrilla in Manilla." Georgie also helped develop great champions in the late seventies and eighties, such as Rocky Lockridge, Pernell Whitaker, Meldrick Taylor, Tyrell Biggs (my brother) and many more. His favorite was Evander Holyfield.

I remember one training camp, hanging around the country club bar where we were lodging, because I knew

Georgie would be sitting there having a drink. He was very talkative when buzzed. My mind was like a sponge, soaking up every drop of boxing knowledge. Every time he'd start off, "That damn Holyfield is gonna make some serious noise." He'd go on and on; I could tell he had a special affection for my brother also, but not in a trainer-fighter way. He appreciated his talents, but felt Tyrell was special in other ways.

I thought about that sparring session and realized how wise Georgie was. Using one word, he restored my confidence, gave me the perfect fight plan and made me realize my potential, instead of a long, drawn-out explanation about utilizing my right hand, step this way or that way, or do this or that. He just went straight to the point. He noticed my lack of confidence, but also my speed and talent. He saw the opening for the right hand. The result: that guy was knocked on his rear, and I realized how I underestimated my abilities.

Another good example of Georgie's style: The day I was being slapped around by middleweight champion John David Jackson's 'frustrating jab' in his gym. After three rounds of jab slapping, I finally pleaded with Georgie, "Man, how the heck can I get around that darn jab?" Those squinty eyes shot back in my direction. He never looked at you directly, but all around you. He calmly said, "Ok, every time he jabs, throw the left hook." I was puzzled again. "That's it?" I asked. He turned, walked away and over his shoulder, replied, "Yeah, and throw it fast." That round I did exactly that and I finally was relieved from the jab assault. It was a perfect example of the old saying 'Talkers rarely do and doers rarely talk'. Georgie, simply, was one of the most down-to-earth, to-the-point guys I've ever met.

Georgie Benton passed away from complications

of pneumonia on Monday morning, September 19, 2011 at the age of 78. He will be truly missed. His spirit will always be alive and strong because he was a master teacher with a powerful style and unforgettable presence.

Bobby "Boogaloo" Watts

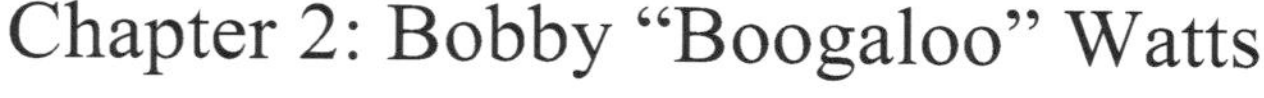

Chapter 2: Bobby "Boogaloo" Watts

Although my nerves were on edge and anxiety was high, I couldn't help but admire the classy and gentlemanly way that Bobby "Boogaloo" Watts handled the small gathering of local reporters and boxing fans interviewing him. An air of content confidence draped across his youthful, boyish face as he took on a barrage of questions, one at a time, with sharp, witty responses.

He was at the weigh-in before my pro debut, and I was so scared I could have puked. But my fear dissolved into intrigue and awe the more I watched Boogaloo's smooth demeanor. He wooed the local press and die-hard Philly boxing fans. I made a mental promise to myself that when I became champion I would carry myself just like Bobby "Boogaloo" Watts when pressed for behind-the-scenes info.

During his interviews I never heard "Boogaloo" say anything derogatory or negative about his opponent. He was confident of victory, for sure, but would lift up his opponent by saying things like, "This fight will be good for him because it will educate him for future challenges and mold him into a champion."

I'd prepared for a four-round preliminary fight on the undercard of Watts' main event as he made a comeback at the 69th Street Forum in Upper Darby, a suburb of my hometown, Philadelphia. I never imagined that only three years later my idol, "Boogaloo" Watts, would hire me as his chief sparring partner and take me under his wing, instructing me on his own tricks and philosophies.

Needless to say, “Boogaloo” smoothly out-boxed his younger opponent in an impressive victory, while I squeaked out a majority draw in a toe-to-toe, blood-and-guts slugfest with some tough Irish kid from Kensington. When I think back now I wish I could have fast-forwarded about three years. I could have used some of “Boogaloo’s” philosophy about over training for my pro debut. “Boogaloo” always told me to train hard, but listen to my body because over-training was worse than under-training.

Bobby “Boogaloo” Watts was a Philadelphia middleweight who established a reputation from the late 60’s to the 80’s as a slick fighter with a smooth, graceful style, which more than likely earned him the nickname “Boogaloo”. He was the first to beat Marvin Hagler in his prime and his name stood among the great Philadelphia middleweights, with the likes of Willie "The Worm" Monroe, Stanley "Kitten" Hayward, Eugene "Cyclone" Hart, "Bad" Bennie Briscoe and more. He was also the cousin of the unctuous heavyweight Jimmy Young.

I loved watching him train. It was so entertaining, especially when he skipped rope. It seemed like a cross between tap dancing and doing the cha-cha. He'd swing the rope in rhythm with his feet. I admit copying this, and mixing that of Sugar Ray Robinson's to create my own style. In fact, an old buddy of mine in the twilight of my boxing career called my skip rope style "sugar-loo".

I learned so much just watching him shadow box. He was older by the time I worked with him and didn't waste any unnecessary movement; everything was precise, to the point. He valued me as a sparring partner because of my speed, telling me that a fighter with speed like that could control any opponent's jab. For him, speed was the key to victory. After each sparring session we'd sit in the locker room of Joe Frazier's gym, and "Boogaloo" would go into depth about boxing philosophy. I cherish those moments to this day. But even more, I cherished the way he would pull his punches and work a lot of defense with me! He was a genuine gentleman of the sport and a huge inspiration to me as a trainer. He encouraged me to promote that same attitude in all of the boxers I've trained.

Simply, being "Boogaloo's" sparring partner was one my most valued times in boxing. He was one of the elite, legendary uncrowned middleweight champions of Philadelphia, and one of the classiest boxers I ever met ... the classy Bobby "Boogaloo" Watts.

To learn more about the incredible career of "Boogaloo" Watts, check out his Wikipedia page. Doghouse Boxing also featured a great interview with him

– not to mention his statistics – on Philly Boxing History. And be sure to watch his legendary fight with Hagler on YouTube.

One thing that's even more exciting is a page we found called "Boogaloo, the Movie", featuring “Boogaloo” talking about his career. Apparently, there’s another film about him in the works, which we're checking into and will get more information as soon as we hear back from the producer.

1984 Olympics

Chapter 3: The First Super Heavyweight Gold Medal Olympic Champion

It was a murky, cloudy evening. The headlights on my burgundy Buick coupe beamed through the light fog as I drove through southwest Philly. One of my favorite past times was cruising in a car with a quality sound system, listening to good, soulful Jazz. The car's confinement and privacy allowed me to soak up the message that only gifted musicians and artists communicate. The music soothed my spirit, altered my mind, allowing me to visualize and meditate about positive outcomes and results. Actually, music was therapeutic during some of my most distraught moments. On this steamy August evening, it was more necessary than ever. I felt terribly anxious and my nerves were on a razor's edge. My mind was in a trance-like daze. My heart rhythmically thumped in my chest. My sweaty hands grasped the steering wheel as I indolently cruised the streets. I was struggling with a lethal combination of high anxiety and deep depression.

I was actually on my way to see an acquaintance, Bobby Dance, whom I befriended several months earlier, stopping by his neighborhood to watch the Olympic Games. My brother Tyrell was competing for amateur boxing's highest prize: the Olympic Super Heavyweight gold medal. I was fortunate enough to find a parking space a few car lengths from Bobby's house. Convenient parking spaces are rare in Philadelphia's neighborhoods of row houses.

Bobby Dance was currently the hottest deejay in Philly. His younger sister, whom I'd also met several months earlier, had a charismatic personality that uplifted my spirits during my most distraught moments. On this evening, I desperately needed a boost. The misty, humid weather was in perfect harmony with my mood.

I was denied the once-in-a-lifetime opportunity to

accompany my brother in Los Angeles as he pursued his Olympic quest. As a service aide employee at the Presbyterian Hospital, management turned down my request for a short leave. My plane ticket and room and board were all accounted for. Some friends urged me to go regardless, but my father pulled some strings to get me hired there. All I could do was pray and hope Tyrell returned victorious. Then, maybe, I could comfortably resign. Almost every day during the trials and box-offs, Tyrell stayed in touch, calling me with updates on training and behind-the- scenes gossip. He was determined to bring me onboard and sympathized with my struggling club-fighter career. As a pro, going solo without a promoter made my career a long shot. I had blind loyalty to my brilliant trainer, Jimmy Arthur, for whom no promoters were willing to do favors.

Jimmy developed the phenomenal Tyrone "Ty the

Fly" Everett but started losing favor with local promoters because of the downhill slide his spirit took after Everett's sudden, tragic murder. Ty was killed just as he was about to go into training for his second shot at the world title after being robbed of the decision during his first attempt. Also, our training gym in south Philly didn't have a strong amateur program. Most who trained there were shrewd street guys motivated by financial gain. Tyrell chose Joe Frazier's Cloverlay Gym in north Philly, which had a strong amateur program and a lot of support from the city and amateur committees. He soon piled up an amateur record of over 100 fights, winning the majority of them, which helped him qualify for the Olympic Games.

But now, an anxious, depressive beast terrorized me. My brother was on the verge of making history this night, and I had to witness it from afar. Depending on his performance, there was a good chance he could change his and our family's lives drastically. Not only would his name be permanently etched in history, there was potential for enormous wealth.

All of these thoughts were racing through my mind and scraping at my soul as I parked down the street from Bobby Dance's house. I had met his sister Carolyn when out enjoying another favorite past time -- partying in Philly's hip clubs. Her stylish, charismatic personality always stimulated me and helped me forget my worries. As I walked toward the door, I could hear Howard Cosell's stern voice blaring from the TV inside the house. Before I raised my hand to knock, the door swung open and there stood Carolyn smiling, inviting me inside. She suddenly spun around and sprinted upstairs, yelling, "I'll be back. The Olympic fights are on TV now." I walked into the living room and spotted Bobby lounging in the chair. I tried to disguise my inner torment with a phony, cool, hip demeanor. "Hey, Bobby, what's happening?" I said. At that time, Bobby's name was ringing pretty loud in the clubs and R&B radio stations around Philly. He had a reputation as being the master of the dance groove and the prince of cool. I had to par with his hipness. He glanced up and responded, "Hey Biggs. Wass up? Been watching the Olympic fights. That darn Meldrick Taylor from North Philly is sure smoking some butts. Your brother's gonna be coming up pretty soon." I took a seat on the sofa across from him and replied, "Yeah, man, I'm all tripped out." He suddenly jerked up in his seat and asked, "How come you are not in L.A. with him, man?" I slumped down in the sofa: "Man, my job wouldn't give me leave time to go." He came back with "Sh_ _, I would've left anyway. This is history being made." My reply: "I know, man, but my father had to really pull some strings to get me that job. So when I do step off, it must be done on legit terms. You know what I mean?" Bobby seemed to understand and replied, "Oh yeah, I can see that. But if Tyrell wins, you'll probably be able to step off and never look back."

I sunk even deeper into the sofa, sighed, murmuring, "Yup, never look back." This was a major lesson I had learned and it changed my entire outlook on life. We were both silent as we watched the TV and listened to Howell Cosell's creative, brassy, but down to earth commentary of the 1984 Olympic Games.

Tyrell's final opponent was Francesco Damiani from Italy. Damiani was 225 pounds of brutal, awkward mayhem. He was an extremely determined brawler who earlier defeated the giant Cuban, Teófilo Stevenson. Stevenson had defeated Tyrell several times in international competitions. This obviously wasn't going to be a walk in the park for Tyrell.

Tyrell was coming off an impressive victory over Lennox Lewis earlier in the box-offs. I remember when I spoke to him the night before his bout with Lennox Lewis and recalled how confident he was; he relieved my concerns by telling me that "He was gonna beat him like his daddy." That made me chuckle because I could remember the beatings we both took from our daddy when we broke the rules. Believe me, those were supreme butt-kickings. I then thought about the next night Tyrell called and this time, that confidence was absent and he seemed somewhat distressed about his sore hands, feeling burnt out and questioning his ability to complete the Olympic tournament. My heart had dropped at this first sign of doubt. This was a rare opportunity to make history, to change his life, to be the first Super Heavyweight Olympic Gold Medal Champion. 1984 was the first year the Super Heavyweight class was recognized in the

Olympic games.

I instinctively proceeded to get in his grill. First I had to remind him that if it were easy it wouldn't be such a great accomplishment. This is the time character and spirit is put to the test to see who is worthy of claiming such a prestigious title. When the going gets tough, the true champion steps out. It's time for the "do or die" attitude. It's all being put on the line now. The one with the most hunger, most will, the most courage, and the most skill will be the one crowned as king in the history books forever.

I had to remind him about the tragic death of our grandmother and how it made our father seem to lose his zeal for life until Tyrell qualified to compete in the Olympic trials. That gave our father new hope and recharged his spirit again. Also, our father had to work two jobs most of our lives to keep us fed, clothed and keep a roof over our heads. I reminded him how our mother came home every evening beat down and worn out from being a special education teacher. Both parents were dealing with these challenges and competing with the destructive lures of the streets of Philly as they raised five children. My older brother, my father's namesake, was constantly back and forth in bouts with hardcore drugs, bringing bitter arguments into our household. Even I had to admit to the headaches I contributed to the whirlwind of stress during my episodes with alcohol and street gangs and other nerve-racking activities I allowed myself to get into as I pranced the streets of West Philly.

Tyrell was silent during my babbling speech. I could sense that he was fixed on every syllable. I eventually ended the heart-felt sermon with "Yo, you gotta do this man. There's no way around it. Do or die." After a brief moment of eerie silence, Tyrell finally responded in a low, steady, but determined voice, "I'm gonna kick his a_ _. I'll call you after the fight." Then he hung up.

I had laid in bed the night prior wide awake, listening to music and visualizing. Hoping and praying God would bless Tyrell with the strength and ability to pull it off. Suddenly, I was popped out of my reflective trance by Bobby Dance's voice "Hey. Your brother's getting ready to go next." I was paralyzed with anxiety as I sat on the sofa peering at the TV as Howard Cosell broke down their bios while the fighters were escorted to the ring by their trainers. This was the most anticipated bout of the evening.

"The Super Heavyweights." Tyrell was bouncing in his corner, looking down, but with a no-joke determination look in his eyes I had never seen before. Damiani was pacing on the other side of the ring and snorting like a starving wolf about to pounce on a meal. My heart was pounding so fast and hard, I wondered if Bobby felt the vibrations from it. The horn finally sounded indicating the beginning of the first round. The two heavyweights charged each other looking to establish their dominance.

Damiani's punches were menacing, looping hooks with very bad intentions. Tyrell shot mostly straight jabs and right hands down the middle with an occasional hook to the head or body; Tyrell's footwork threw Damiani a little off balance as they traded combinations. You could hear the excitement in Howard Cosell's voice as he gave his prediction of who he thought won the first round. Although he had Tyrell slightly ahead, I still felt like it was too close to call and it could've gone either way. The second round was almost exactly like the first round. Damiani's determination sure wasn't making things any easier. The winner of this bout would obviously have to take the third round big. By now the anxiety had me numb as it vise-gripped my insides.

The TV camera zoomed in on Tyrell's corner and I noticed a wild look in his eyes that I had never seen before. I thought about the lecture I gave him the night before. I thought about his sore hands and broken down body. I knew all that was left inside was will and spirit. The look in his eyes clearly said, "Do or Die". Finally the horn for the third round went off. I felt my body tremble from the adrenaline. Damiani's trainer must've told Damiani he was behind and needed to win that third round to be victorious because he stormed out of his corner like his life depended on it. But Tyrell met him in the middle of the ring with the same kind of determination. Now there was over 450 pounds of Super Heavyweight brutal perpetual motion. Damiani was a windmill of menacing haymakers as Tyrell exploded nonstop combinations with head movement and angles. By the end of the round, Howard

Cosell's excitement made him abandon all of his composure as he screamed the blow-by-blow action. It was clear the two Super Heavyweights were exhausted and were driven by will alone. Tyrell appeared to end his punch exchanges with an extra jab or hook. The round finally came to an end. Now the anxiety was higher than ever before as we nervously awaited the judges' decision as to who was the winner of the explosive Super Heavyweight Gold Medal Championship bout.

As the judges tallied the scores, you could've heard an ant burp. The referee finally ordered the Super Heavyweight contestants to the middle of the ring. He grabbed both of their wrists in anticipation of the judges' nod so he could raise the hand of the winner. Tyrell uncontrollably did a "jogging in place" dance with his head held down, bracing for the final decision. I thought I was going to crap a golden brick.

After an excruciating moment that felt like an eternity, the referee announced "And the winner is Ty...". Before he could finish Tyrell's name, Tyrell, consumed by utter excitement, snatched his arm away from the referee and did a victory leap that would've made you wonder if he won the gold medal for the high jump rather than boxing. I was dizzy from the flood of emotions that consumed me. Bobby Dance was so excited he screamed "WOOOOOOOO." Carolyn raced half way down the stairs screaming, "What happened? Did he win? Did he win?" All Bobby could say was "WOOOOOO" again. I stood up on unsteady legs with misty eyes and somehow managed to blurt out "He did it. He did it." Then I turned and zombie-walked toward the door. I had to get out of there fast. My coolness was at stake here. I couldn't have reached the door sooner because by then a levee had burst and a flood of tears drenched my face. I finally made it to my car and collapsed over the steering wheel, heaving tears of emotion that I had never experienced before in my whole life. I looked up and noticed Carolyn standing in the doorway staring with expressed concern. I pulled off and tapped the horn of my car in acknowledgment. She waved in response, still watching as I drove out of view. More tears gushed as I drove through the blanket of fog towards my apartment. I just kept saying over and over. "He did it. He did it. My younger brother is the Olympic Gold Medal Super Heavyweight Champion. The first in history to claim that title."

Although I did notice some boos when his hand was raised in victory, the impact was still intoxicating. I thought about how funny life is because Tyrell was the one most unlikely to be the one to claim the title. Growing up in West Philly he was known as "Burt", the laid back, easy going, big teddy bear that loved to make people laugh, and he had a special knack of doing it well. He had managed to side step the trouble and street gangs, for which the streets of Philadelphia were notoriously known.

Tyrell rarely got into fights and everyone seemed to genuinely like him. He was an extremely talented basketball player and was on the best high school basketball team in the country during the late seventies. He was encouraged to box by my father, a bonafide boxing fan who had boxed in the army. Also, I believe my club fighting boxing career might have added a little to his motivation. His boxing talent was evident in his very first amateur bout as he easily out-pointed his opponent with little effort and with a style reminiscent of the great Muhammad Ali.

I remembered how our father use to take us to the fights at the spectrum in South Philadelphia where we would be mesmerized by the old Philly greats such as

"Bad" Benny Briscoe, Willie "The Worm" Monroe, Bobby "Boogaloo" Watts, "Cyclone" Hart and many more. Tyrell and I use to be wide-eyed and astonished by these bigger than life figures that tickled my father's fancy like anything we've never seen before. Now "Burt" was the Super Heavyweight Olympic Gold Medal Champion of the world. Lonnie Liston Smith's "Quiet Moments" oozed out of my stereo speakers in my car as I slowly cruised through the streets of West Philly in a hypnotic trance of ecstasy as I soaked in the reality of this night's history making event. God had surely graced our family this evening.

When I arrived at my apartment, my phone was ringing. I rushed in and answered the phone. It was Carolyn asking me if I was all right. I answered, "Sure. I'm fine. I just got overwhelmed there for a minute. I'm gonna get back with you later so we can celebrate."

Before she could reply, the incoming call tone beeped through. Anxious to take the call, I asked her to hold and pressed the answer button on the phone. Through all the partying noise in the background I heard Tyrell screaming to me "You seen it? You seen it? I did it." My body felt all tingly and my eyes got misty again when I answered, "Yeah man, you did it. It was beautiful." Then he said "Yo man, Imma call you later or maybe tomorrow and tell you all about it. Imma go kick it wit mom and dad now." I hung up the phone and collapsed backwards on the bed and just laid there in the darkness for the rest of the night, visualizing and convincing myself that this was real and not a dream.

The next few weeks were crammed with celebrations and parades; Tyrell even went to Washington D.C. and met President Ronald Reagan at the White House.

One evening, about a month later, I was laying in bed chilling and cracking up watching "The Honeymooners" on TV when the phone rang. I answered and was surprised to hear the voice of Shelly Finkel on the other end. Shelly Finkel was a successful promoter who helped promote the famous rock concert "Woodstock" and now he was promoting and managing world-class boxers. He had teamed up with the famous boxing manager Lou Duva and signed my brother, Tyrell, and the other gold medal champions, Mark Breland, Pernell Whitaker, Meldrick Taylor and bronze medal champion Evander Holyfield from the 1984 team. It was time for them to turn Pro and Shelly was asking me to report to their training camp. I had already turned in my resignation letter to the administration at my job a week earlier when Tyrell asked me to accompany him in his quest to win the world heavyweight championship once he turned pro. Of course,

I was more than ready for this mission. It was totally a dream come true.

After I hung up the phone, I lied back on the bed, turned on the jazz and went into another meditation. As exciting as things were looking at that moment, there was no way of telling what crazy dramatics and wild experiences were in store for me during the upcoming boxing endeavors. Although I had some pretty stimulating experiences as a pro-boxer on the club fight scene in Philly for several years, I was about to take it to the world class level now and the adventures and dramatics would be escalated one hundred fold.

Yep, it was time to fasten my seatbelt and get prepared for a wild roller coaster ride of storybook adventures in the cut-throat, but stimulating world of professional boxing.

Rocky Lockridge

Chapter 4: The Honor of a True Champion

Rocky Lockridge

It was always a stimulating experience for me to stroll down 60th Street in West Philadelphia. Usually on pleasant days, I would park my car and ride on public transportation to the gym. I would have to walk up 60th Street to catch the el, a high- speed public rail line that stretched across one end of Philly to the other. Then I would catch the Broad Street subway to South Philly (little Italy), where the boxing gym was located.

60th Street was always crowded and busy. The chatter from the variety of merchants, corner boys, winos and everyday working people, along with the impatient honking of passing cars and occasional sirens of racing police cars were like music to my ears on this particular day.

I was feeling real light on my feet and all my

movement seemed so effortless. My senses seemed heightened and reflexes felt cat-like keen. It was like I could snatch a flying gnat out of the air.

Yes, on this day I was feeling dynamite, mentally, physically and spiritually, because I was in pretty good shape. I use to hear the old-timers say "with boxing, you gotta get in shape to get in shape." At this moment, I was experiencing exactly that. Everything was really peaking.

As I walked by a familiar group of local corner boys, one of them hollered out, "Hey Stick! What's up man?" (My older brother nicknamed me "Stick" because of the bony frame I had as a teenager. I hollered back "Everything's good man. Just got a few rounds in with Rocky Lockridge today at the gym."

The haters in the group scowled at me in disbelief while the rest of the gang gawked in awe. Rocky Lockridge was the current Junior Lightweight Champion who had fought memorable 15 round battles with the legendary Mexican Champion, Julio Cesar Chavez and the great Featherweight Champion from Panama, Eusebio Pedroza. That day I had just spent 5 good sparring rounds with Rocky, which added a significant boost to my confidence.

Coming up on the fast streets of Philly, it was almost impossible not to have your share of experiences with drugs and alcohol, which I did, but nothing can compare to the natural high of being in peak shape, and especially in peak boxing shape.

I had several years of boxing experience under my belt and those years were challenging. But now all the blood, sweat, and tears that came with the training were finally starting to pay off. My body was now hard and tough, with very little fat, with toned muscles and my confidence was escalated with my acknowledgement of my new found self-defense capabilities.

The ring generalship and skill had qualified me to be able to hold my own against some of the local boxers and champions of that era that were close to my weight class. That day I was giving the great Rocky Lockridge sparring rounds, helping him prepare for an upcoming title defense.

Although the Passyunk Gym in South Philly is where I got my start, and where I did most of my training, I had occasional stints at Champs Gym on 24th and Columbia Avenue in North Philly, where I was briefly under the tutelage of the legendary Quenzell McCall. I also frequented Joe Frazier's gym at Broad and Lehigh in North Philly, where I sparred with the classy and great Bobby "Boogaloo" Watts. And it was Georgie Benton's gym at 16th and Stiles Street where I traded sparring rounds with such great champions such as John David Jackson, Meldrick Taylor, and Rocky Lockridge.

I remember at that time I was in peak shape and scheduled to meet Rocky Lockridge for more sparring at Georgie's gym. My conditioning and confidence made me eagerly anticipate the session. When that day finally arrived, I came to the gym earlier than usual and shadowboxed and danced around the ring to the funky music that was kicking from the high-powered boom box in the corner of the gym.

After 30 minutes, Rocky came strolling in carrying his bag and shot a curious glance at me as he made his way toward the locker room to change. I enthusiastically shouted at him "What's up Rock!" He just nodded his head, waved and went about his business.

Now I went into top gear shooting fast combinations in the air. You would've thought I was the champion and "Rocky Lockridge" was my sparring partner. After a while, Rocky came back and sat down so Georgie could wrap his hands. All this time he was watching me with a curious look on his face. I had endless energy so I showed off my footwork and my quick combination improvisations. Man, I was really tripping. Eventually Georgie finished the hand wrapping and Rocky got up to shadowbox and warm up. Georgie stood and looked over at me and grunted with his raspy voice, "You got five in you today, baby cakes?" I answered back "Yeah man, maybe six." All the time Rocky was just nonchalantly shadowboxing. Yep, I was in the process of making a real stupid mistake from which I would learn a powerful lesson to take with me for the rest of my career in boxing.

When we started gearing up for sparring, I was so jumpy Georgie had to scold me to "be still" so he could tie my gloves. Rocky just kept giving me that curious look. Rocky Lockridge was a junior lightweight champion that fought most of the best in his weight class and sported more than 300 amateur fights before he turned pro, winning most of them. (His pro record was 44-9-0.) Rocky was one of the stars of Lou Duva's stable of the tomorrow's champion crew consisting of top ranked middleweight "Alex Ramos", junior welterweight champ Johnny "Bump City" Bumphus and more. I was just a local pro-club fighter with only a few fights under my belt, and I was acting like a superstar. The first round went pretty smooth as Rocky and I sharp shot each other as we were feeling each other out. I was feeling so good, I came out the second round with a blazing combination, then did a Jersey-Joe cake walk and grabbed the rope, dropped my other hand and slipped Rocky a right-hand "Gypsy Joe" style. I shook my shoulders and danced back to the middle of the ring.

Georgie just watched silently. Maybe he was a little entertained by my ring antics, or what the old timers used to call ‘getting cute’, but I didn’t think Rocky was too entertained when I saw that familiar curious look in his eye right before he delivered a menacing straight right hand corkscrew punch to my ribs. Now the show was over as I dropped to my knees from the pain. Rocky suddenly rushed to my aid in concern and asked “Yo man, you alright?” I said, “I’m cool man. I’m cool.” But I really wasn’t. I was embarrassed, humiliated and I thought my ribs were broken. I finished the next three rounds like a deer in the headlights. At least Rocky was merciful enough not to throw any more right hands at my ribs.

After the sparring session, I moseyed over to the side of the gym nursing my aching ribs. I sat there and admired the way Rocky shadowboxed to the R&B rhythms kicking out of the boom box. He always shadowboxed with his gloves on after sparring sessions. As I sat there cringing from the pain of my ribs, it suddenly dawned on me that all these sparring sessions with Rocky had gone to my head. Rocky had been holding back all those times, and on this day, when I decided to 'get cute', he brought me back down to earth and let me know who the real champ was. It only took that look in his eye and that one punch to my ribs to give me two weeks of excruciating pain and a rude awakening to the true honor of a champion.

The more I thought about it, I admired and respected Rocky Lockridge even more. In all our sessions, Rocky just toyed with me and pulled his punches for the purpose of sharpening his arsenal of tools for the real battle, and at the same time salvaging my ego, dignity and health. He was capable of destroying me within two rounds and that cork-screw right hand to my ribs was an eye-opening message that said, "I'll allow you to sharp-shoot with me so I can polish my skills and you can continue to learn, but don't ever forget who the real champ is and always show the proper respect because I paid some serious dues to get it".

Now don't get me wrong, Rocky Lockridge was a mellow, soft-spoken gentleman always quick to smile, but in the ring he was a beast. I remember when I first observed him at the Spectrum in Philadelphia. I think

his record was around 6 or 7 to 0. I remember how amazed I was at seeing him batter his opponent methodically and effortlessly in about 2 ½ rounds and barely breaking a sweat. I was still in the infant stage of an ambitious amateur career and right at that moment I was mentally recording some of Rocky's stuff so I could add to my own growing weaponry for the ring.

Now I was able to really acknowledge the honor in this great champion as I recalled the very first time I personally met "Rocky". It was dollar night at Chuck's, a hip night club and Discotheque on Broad Street in Philly, where the infamous Broad Street Bullies DJs creatively spun the hottest and latest tunes to help attract the hipsters from all over Germantown, North Philly, South Philly, West Philly and some from nearby New Jersey.

During my early boxing years, Chuck's was one of my favorite Monday night hangouts. On this particular Monday night I was hypnotized with euphoria as I danced to this real saucy funky tune the DJ was kicking. It got so good to me that I attempted an about-face spin to my dance moves and crashed head-on with some short cat dancing beside me. The impact was so hard that I knocked his glasses crooked, hanging off his face. I immediately grabbed him and apologized, hoping to squash any potential for a brawl. I said "Yo man, you alright? It was my fault." The short dude just stepped back and gently re-adjusted his glasses and politely responded saying "Naw, don't worry about it. I was caught up in the music and wasn't paying attention either." He smiled, turned and resumed his funky moves with his hipped up dance partner. His smile sparked my memory and right then it hit me. I blurted "Yo, Rocky Lockridge!! You're Rocky Lockridge. Yo, wassup CHAMP!!! Yo man I remember seeing your fight at the Spectrum. Man you got some sleeping pills in your fist." He half blushed and half grinned and said "Wassup Partner. Good to meet you. What's your name?" I excitedly responded "I'm Biggs – Xavier Biggs. I box out of Passyunk Gym in South Philly under Jimmy Arthur." His eyes opened wider and said "Oh, yeah. Cool. I know Art. Excellent trainer." As we were still swaying to the rhythm of the music and chatting, I noticed our frustrated dance partners had eased off into the crowd. I was just excited to meet the great Junior Lightweight Champion Rocky Lockridge face to face and he was probably glad to kick it with somebody because we were both hanging out 'solo'.

We broke away from the dance floor and went to the bar and had some light drinks and sparked up a friendly chat. It was really cool to hang out with the champ at Chuck's, but it was even cooler that he was gentleman enough not to kick my butt for crashing into him on the dance floor. Although Chuck's was crawling with stylish, fashionable hipsters, Rocky kind of stuck out with his conservative, college boy, geek style. One would've never guessed that he was one of the most feared and dominating world champions in the junior lightweight division.

This Rocky Lockridge story was one of many episodes in my boxing career that helped me understand the honor of a true champion. The collision on the dance floor at Chuck's and all those controlled rounds of sparring proved Rocky's honor. He could've easily destroyed me in sparring and if he would've had a chip on his shoulder, I would have been sucking my food from a straw after the dance floor collision. But Rocky was a man content with himself and confident in his abilities. He had nothing to prove. Also, he was disciplined enough to think things through before he allowed emotions to dictate his actions. Boxing has a tendency to do that to men. I guess that is why it is sometimes known as the 'gentlemen's sport' despite the stereotypical image boxing may portray.

I have never been in any place where I have seen men respect each other more than in a boxing gym. I have operated five boxing gyms and I've always noticed that

no matter what race, religion or culture, everyone was always treated with equal respect and there was very little riffraff. Of course, there were rare exceptions of some knuckleheads who were unsure of themselves and had something to prove, but they would be quickly excused from the gym. I must say this was one of the major reasons why I had to break ties with some of the boxers I trained.

Honor and integrity were strict policies in my gyms and I didn't tolerate anything less than that. Although some of the new trainees would have a tendency to slip off their square and explore the arrogant, 'trying to prove something route', I would immediately throw down a serious lecture on honor. If they didn't bite, they were eventually escorted from the gym. Almost all of the world-class boxers and champions I worked with always seem to be mellow, well mannered and respectful, and were the first to walk away from any potential altercation. They never seem to take advantage of less skilled or less experienced boxers in sparring. They might have to touch them here or there to keep less talented sparring partners honest, but never in an abusive way. I'm drawn closer and more motivated to help boxers with that mentality.

Because of the violent nature of the sport of boxing, it is extremely important for the participants to carry themselves with a sense of honor and integrity, especially the champions. You do have some boxers that were trained since the beginning of their careers to be aggressive and all they know is one speed. But even those guys were the sweetest, nicest people you ever met outside of the ring.

Today, my top amateur boxer and top pro boxer (with whom I share training duties) are the perfect examples. "Kitten" Carlos Monroe, the 17-year old 6-time State Golden Glove Champion, is the most mellow, respectful gentleman you will ever meet. "King" Zahir Raheem, 1996 Bronze Medal Olympic Champion and 4-time professional champion, is a 'quick to smile and laugh' gentleman that treats everyone from the greenest amateur to a has-been pro with the utmost respect and never abuses or takes advantage of less talented or inexperienced sparring partners.

In my view, growing up on the tough streets of Philly and given my succeeding journeys in boxing, the most dangerous and capable men were the most laid back and the most humble. They were willing to walk away from trouble; but the ones that were quick to buck-up and flap off their mouths were the ones that were insecure and desperate to prove something. Maybe if there were more boxing gyms in the inner cities, there would be less violence in the streets. Perhaps we all could learn a lesson by acknowledging the honor of true champions.

Chapter 5: Night of the Incredible Jab
Tyrell Biggs

As the 747 touched down at the Airport in Reno, Nevada memories of my last visit to Reno consumed my mind. The first time I was there, it was to aid my brother Tyrell in his quest to capture the world amateur heavyweight championship from Teófilo Stevenson, the big Cuban who had dominated that title for several years prior. Before the fight we had spent a few weeks in Detroit where Tyrell was under the tutelage of Emanuel Stuart in preparation for the championship bout.

While we were in Detroit I shared a room in one of Emanuel's homes with Frank Tate. Frank later qualified for the 1984 Olympic team and won a Gold Medal. Later as a pro he became a Middleweight World Champion. It was an incredible experience just being there with so many great fighters. I spent a lot of time hanging out with now deceased Steve McCrory who also made the 1984 team. He also went on to become a Gold Medal Champion.

When we arrived in Reno for the amateur championships, I shared a room with Evander Holyfield. Even back then Evander was known for his no nonsense determination and incredible will. He won a Bronze Medal at the '84 Olympics and there is no need to even mention all he has done as a pro.

But the most prominent memory is Tyrell's amateur championship fight with Stevenson. I felt chills run up my spine as I reminisced seeing Tyrell collapse in pain from a body shot delivered by Stevenson. Even before the body shot I had noticed a lack of effort from Tyrell. Something had put the brakes on for him and I could see that it was more mental than physical. How could he not be inspired after sharing training camp in Detroit with all those champions? It was incredible – Thomas Hearns, Wilfred Benitez, and Matt Saad Muhammad all graced the canvas while we were there. There was definitely something going on in his head, but I couldn't figure out what it was. The only thing I knew was after that night Tyrell would lose a lot of respect from the fans and the sports writers. All these memories flooded my mind as we taxied down the runway to the terminal gate at the Reno airport for the second time.

I never would have imagined that our second visit to Reno would turn everything around for Tyrell and silence his worst critics. In the boxing world Tyrell would forever be known for this night. Whether a young beginning amateur or a salty old veteran of boxing, Tyrell would from then on be remembered in this fight with the utmost respect.

Weigh-ins can be pretty scary because they are a harsh reality of what is about to take place. The participants are checked out and the contest is made to be official. A lot of fights are won and lost at the weigh-in. I was always amazed at how cool and nonchalant Tyrell always appeared to be at this initial meeting of his opponent. He was usually the one to break the tension by cracking jokes and clowning around, especially when Mark Breland, Pernell Whitaker, or Meldrick Taylor were present. Tyrell was the clown of the crew and they were the ones who laughed and enjoyed his frolics the most.

On this second visit to Reno, things were pretty different at the weigh-in. It was an intriguing heavyweight match between Tyrell and top rated heavyweight Jeff Sims. Jeff could be any boxer's worst nightmare. His unusually large hands fit his unusually large reputation as a fearless brutal knockout puncher, and he seemed to take pleasure in inflicting punishment. His pro record was 22-3 with 21 KO's and most of his victims took a dive face first. During the weigh-in Sims harshly talked crap and tried to belittle Tyrell. He appeared confident that he would win, assured by his impressive KO rate, having already KO'ed former champions, top contenders, and upcoming hopefuls. Tyrell seemed a little on edge for this one. He wasn't cracking as many jokes and I noticed a look of concern in his eyes.

After the weigh-in we went back to our room and Tyrell complained, "Why did they put me in there with this crazy guy?" I responded by telling him not to focus on how crazy the guy is, but to focus on how to use his talent and skills to defeat him. I told Tyrell his marquee value would sky-rocket once he defeated Sims. In my opinion, if Tyrell wasn't capable of out-boxing Sims the match wouldn't have been made. He would just have to focus and utilize his abilities.

Tyrell just laid there staring at the ceiling for a moment then turned his back to me and seemed to drift off to sleep. I reached over from the other bed and flicked the light off and turned my back to him, but my eyes were wide open and my heart was pounding a nervous rapid beat as I wondered whether this fight was lost at the weigh-in.

The next evening at the venue Tyrell seemed more relaxed and loose as he warmed up in the dressing room with Georgie Benton going over the fight plan. Lou Duva was reminding Tyrell that he had the best jab in the business.

Jeff Sims entered the ring to a title wave of "boos"

from the audience. He circled around the ring mouthing off to the press and commentators. A few weeks before, I had designed Tyrell's robe for the fight and requested that the words "Mr. Biggs" be embroidered on the back. I did that thinking that when you refer to a man's name with "Mister" in front it indicated respect. In the time since his professional debut Tyrell had conquered a lot to warrant respect. He had overcome a serious crack addiction and never relapsed; he had run up a string of knockouts after being criticized as a fighter who didn't have a punch. His respect had been earned. Ironically, this night would earn him even more respect than he could have ever imagined.

The first round of the fight Tyrell boxed brilliantly like he was sending Sims a message, "You don't scare me." But all that changed in the second round, when Sims came out determined to break Tyrell's will, whistling menacing combinations with a fervor. Tyrell was doing what old-time trainers in Philly used to call, "dealing with it." He dealt with it until a brutal Sims right hand caught Tyrell on the right collar bone and sent him reeling into the ropes. When the bell rang ending the 2nd round, Tyrell retreated to his corner looking down at his right shoulder in concern. I could see that something was wrong.

At the start of the third round Tyrell attempted to shoot a straight right hand at Sims and stopped it midway, grasped his right collarbone, and started back peddling. Now I was concerned something was really wrong and I clutched Meldrick Taylor's forearm and screamed "Something's wrong with his right shoulder man!" Meldrick and Evander Holyfield were sitting ringside silent and wide eyed in astonishment. Excitement and tension were at a fever pitch in the arena now as Tyrell back peddled flicking an assortment of jabs at Sims keeping him off balance to slow the furious and relentless attack in front of him. I heard Lou Duva screaming “Use that jab baby, use that jab!”

Georgie Benton targeted Tyrell’s confidence as he pleaded with Tyrell, “This guy is nothing! You can outbox him!” Jeff Sims grew more determined and vicious like a shark that smelled blood and by the 4th round Meldrick and Evander had joined in with Lou screaming, “Use the jab!” There were moments that it looked like Tyrell was succumbing to Sims’ onslaught, but miraculously he would soak up some confidence from somewhere and start displaying the sweet science like I’ve never seen it before, especially by a heavyweight. Tyrell was gaining control of the fight.

Tyrell kept using the jab to keep Sims off balance. He was slipping, sliding and ducking Sims’ arsenal of menacing combinations, frustrating Sims. As the rounds wore on Tyrell’s jabs started turning into hooks to the head and body, and uppercuts, peppering Sims at every off-balanced turn. The whole arena was in a frenzy of tension and excitement! Even the boxing officials and TV commentators were sweating bullets at the sight of Tyrell's incredible concentration and determination that was required to handle the excruciating pressure of Sims. By the last rounds Tyrell was taking his one-handed fight to Sims dominating the fight. Commentator Alex Wallau, one of Tyrell's worst critics, was now singing his praises. Jim Lampley, now an HBO analyst, grinned with admiration. At the end of the crazy high voltage fight, Tyrell's hands were raised in victory with a unanimous decision; he had fought the last 8 rounds with only a left hand and a broken right collarbone.

Jeff Sims had been one of the most fearsome and dangerous heavyweights and Tyrell had defeated him with only one hand. With only eight professional fights to his credit and in his first ten round fight, the statement Tyrell had made was deafening. Tyrell had earned the name "Mr. Biggs".

As Tyrell pounced around the ring with his arms raised in victory, I waited until he was close and I whispered to him, "This night was meant to be." He turned and whispered back, "Yeah, it sure was." and then he was gone, continuing his victory prance around the ring.

Later that evening I excused myself early from the victory celebration dinner (Lou Duva was famous for arranging victory dinners after fights) and I headed to my hotel room thinking to myself, "I see why men treasure their respect so much . . . you really have to pay some heavy dues to get it."

Now I can look back to the first visit to Reno and the amateur title fight with Stevenson, the crack addiction ordeal my brother went through, and the ruthless critics. I understand now that every time you overcome an obstacle with the right attitude and determination you become stronger and more prepared to conquer even bigger obstacles. When you've done that, you will achieve greatness. My brother had just beaten one of the best punchers in the heavyweight division fighting with one hand and a broken collar bone. He had achieved greatness that would never be forgotten.

I got to my hotel room and flopped onto the bed. I was emotionally exhausted. I've been through some ordeals coming up on the streets in Philly, but I can't recall any experience that would come close to the level of drama and excitement I had experienced on that night. I thanked God for this incredible victory. What a night. What a fight. It was the night of the incredible jab, but perhaps more fitting, it was the night of the incredible heart.

MELDRICK TAYLOR

Chapter 6: Meldrick "TNT" Taylor

Grossinger's, a lavish Jewish resort hidden in the Catskills in upstate New York, opened in 1919, became a famous landmark when it was chosen as training headquarters for Rocky Marciano, Joe Louis, Sugar Ray Robinson and other world-class boxers. The twin attributes of seclusion and high altitude, along with the accommodations made Grossinger's a favorite training camp.

In 1984, Lou Duva, Shelly Finkel and Main Events chose Grossinger's as the training camp to prepare the five 1984 American Olympic boxing medalists for their professional debut. The youngest of the five, 17 year old featherweight Meldrick Taylor, was the youngest boxer ever to win an Olympic gold medal.

The others were: Pernell (Sweet Pea) Whitaker, the slick, sharp shooting, defensive wizard and lightweight gold medalist; Mark Breland, a tall, rangy, welterweight gold medalist from New York; Evander (The Real Deal) Holyfield, the iron-willed, rock-hard human weapon and heavyweight bronze medal champion; and, my brother, Tyrell Biggs, the first super heavyweight to win a gold medal and the only American to this date to hold the title.

In a gracious and compassionate gesture, Tyrell invited me to come to camp with him as his aide and assistant. Tyrell knew the frustrations I had experienced as a struggling Philly club fighter.

Lou Duva and Shelly Finkel agreed and thought it was a good idea to have me around to help out and be a source of motivation. Later they would find me to be more useful in other ways.

Early one brisk fall morning, I decided to join in the morning roadwork. We all started jogging together, but after about a mile, I began lagging behind, panting and gasping for air, as the others gradually disappeared ahead of me. The 1984 Olympic class was obviously adjusted to the high altitude as a result of the time spent training in Colorado Springs.

I slowed my pace to a "Bad Bennie Briscoe" jog to allow everyone else to get out of sight then turned around and went back to my hotel room and collapsed on the bed for a well deserved power nap. An hour later, I was awakened by a hard pounding and opened the door to an agitated Lou Duva. Right away he blurted "Hey Xavier, you had some fights, right? You feel up to giving Meldrick a few rounds?" I replied "Yeah. Sure I'll give the kid a little work." Lou gave me a funny look and left saying over his shoulder "Okay good. Meet you at the gym at 11:30." I would later learn the meaning of that funny look.

At this point I was thinking there was nothing Meldrick could show me that I haven't already seen. After all, I had been a pro for several years and he was training to make his pro debut. Also, at home I had held my own in sparring with some of the local big name Philly fighters such as Robert Hines, Buster Drayton and Mike Rossman, and they were all bigger than me. I was a welterweight in my early twenties and Meldrick was just a 17 year old featherweight trying to move up to lightweight. I obviously thought the odds would be in my favor and that accounted for my cocky response to Lou's request for me to spar with Meldrick.

I promptly arrived at the gym at 11:30. Meldrick was already there with his protective cup on and shadowboxing in the ring. I think I might have irked Georgie Benton and Tommie Brooks as I took my own sweet time to warm up. Even Meldrick did not seem to acknowledge me as he warmed up in the ring. When we finally started putting on the equipment to spar, Tommy Brooks quizzed me about my experience as he laced my gloves up. I assured him I was very capable of handling myself. He just gave me that same puzzled look Lou Duva had given me earlier. On entering the ring I started bouncing around in my corner to get my rhythm and loosen up while waiting for Georgie to signal the beginning of the round. I looked over at Meldrick and noticed he was glaring at me with a look in his eyes that implied "I'm going to hurt you." Growing up on the streets of Philly, I learned it was always better to keep your cool under a tough guy raft, so I acted as if I wasn't fazed.

Georgie finally screamed "time" and like brown-skinned lightning, Meldrick darted across the ring and immediately sent a fast right-hand to the bridge of my nose before I could lift my hands. He then commenced to pounding my mid-section with rapid combinations. Through the pain and stars circling inside my head, I realized Meldrick had incredible hand speed and power. The only choices were to quit or try and fight him off.

I managed to get one of my signature left hooks through his defense, which made him blink. But I paid dearly for it when he peppered me with a tornado of rapid body shots. Finally Georgie screamed “time” signaling the end of the round. Meldrick retreated to his corner with his hands raised in victory while I staggered back to my corner like an old Philly wino with a bad hangover.

I stared at Tommy Brooks with a silly smirk on my face as he scolded me for trading punches with Meldrick. “Time” Georgie screamed again to start the second round. When I turned around, Meldrick was already there to feed my face with some hard left jabs. I made a pathetic attempt to do a Muhammad Ali shuffle to try to avoid him but his speed and strength was overwhelming.

By the third round, I had finally got some control of my faculties and actually put up a little competition. Meldrick, however, again raised his hands in victory after the third round as if he just won a fight.

After spending several years fighting in gyms in Philly and now seeing firsthand the difference between a club fighter and a world-class boxer, I learned although skill and talent play an important part, it is self-confidence and the unrelenting determination to win that takes a fighter to the top.

We had only sparred three rounds and to me it felt like ten. When I stumbled out of the ring, I looked around the gym glaring at everyone to let them know I was alright and had held my own. The other fighters just looked at me with pity in their eyes and continued their gym work.

As I exited the ring, Meldrick started working hand pads with his first trainer, Willie Rush. This was my first real impression of observing good pad work. Meldrick's speed and power on Rush's pads sounded like machine gun fire, only in a better rhythm.

Later I learned why Lou Duva asked me to spar with

Meldrick. Meldrick had sent all of his sparring partners home prematurely with broken noses and/or ribs and had no one left.

Later, Meldrick Taylor, along with the others, made his pro debut in November 1984 at the Felt Forum inside Madison Square Garden. He demolished his opponent in the first round; his opponent was a pro with over ten fights and a winning record. This made me feel good about having sparred with Meldrick. I had survived three rounds and had not been sent home with any broken bones.

Meldrick later went on to become a World Champion in two weight divisions. In September 1988, he won the IBF world junior welterweight title. In January, 1991, he won the WBA world welterweight title and in 1990, Ring Magazine rated his fight with Julio Cesar Chavez as the fight of the year. Meldrick retired from the ring in 2002. He has written an autobiography *Two*

Seconds from Glory, which is to be made into a movie.

Meldrick and I became good friends and despite the beating he gave me in the ring, I learned that outside the ring he was a mild-mannered gentleman. Meldrick Taylor was part of the greatest U.S. Olympic boxing team in history.

REMATCH OF THE YEAR
TUES. APR. 6 8 P.M.
CYCLONE
HART
BENNIE
BRISCOE
Spectrum
PHILA. ARENA BOXING
TUES. MAR 21
BENNIE BRISCOE
JORGE ROSALES
BILLY DOUGLAS
CARLOS MARKS
RETURN OF THE PUNCHERS
SPECTRUM FIGHTS!
WED. MAY
P.M.
ROSSMAN
BRISCOE
MEDINA
BALDWIN
JOHNSON
Spectrum
BENNIE BRISCOE
BENNIE
BRISCOE
A TRIBUTE
MONDAY NIGHT FIGHTS!
MON. JAN. 29, 8 P.M.
BENNIE BRISCOE
CARLOS SALINAS
THREE PRELIMINARY BOUTS
Spectrum

Chapter 7: "Bad" Bennie Briscoe (1943-2010) by Terri Moss

"Bad" Bennie Briscoe passed away on December 29, 2010, in a Philadelphia hospice, aged 67, with his wife by his side. The Georgia-born, Philadelphia-raised Briscoe had a 66-24-5 record with 53 knockouts in a career spanning from 1966 to 1982. He is a Philly icon, the greatest uncrowned champion known to the city (though there were several), one of those fighters whose style has been an example for up-and-coming stars. I say that because even though he began his boxing career before I was born, I know all about him. From eight years of training with Xavier Biggs, I can honestly say that I've heard the name "Bennie Briscoe" hundreds of times. We have combinations named after him. We have fighting strategies named after him. And we even have 'roadwork' named after him. Countless times I'd hear Biggs say; "Bennie Briscoe!" and I knew what that meant: Pick it up! Let those hands go! Pressure! Power shots!

It wore me out. And when it was time for a run: "Not too much…just do a Bennie Briscoe around the pond." According to Biggs, Bennie was always running around what is now called Kelly Drive in Philadelphia. "Hey, there goes Bennie Briscoe!" was often heard on his daily, ten-mile trot -- the same trot used for his 'ring walk'. The same trot used to stalk opponents. Bennie Briscoe, a Philadelphia icon, the legend. I wish I could have seen him before he passed away.

I named my cat after him a few years ago. (How funny -- only it's a girl, so I call her "Betty Briscoe"). Bennie has been a big part of my boxing career and I incorporate his styles to train my fighters, just as Xavier did with me and his fighters. Bennie has been passed down like a family heirloom in boxing.

Thank goodness for YouTube. That's where I've seen him most, along with the other greats: Eugene Hart, Carlos Monzon, Marvin Hagler, Emile Griffith, Teddy Mann, Ralph Hollett, Rodrigo Valdez, Tony Mundine, Tony Chiaverini, Vito Antuofermo, Eddie Mustafa Muhammad, Carlos Mark, Carlos Salinas and Juarez De Lima II.

Fights like Bennie's with Marvin Hagler are hard to come by these days. He was incredible in his prime and, when older, gave young fighters a lesson they wouldn't forget. It would have been really cool to meet and honor him at one of my Atlanta Corporate Fight Night events. I'm sure he got a lot of recognition in Philly. Everyone loved "Bad" Bennie Briscoe.

You can see one of my favorite Bennie fights on YouTube, versus Al Quinney in 1972. Bennie was such a viscous puncher; he destroyed Quinney in the second of a scheduled 10-rounder.

Check out his fights if you haven't before. He's one of the greats from the golden years of boxing and should be studied and appreciated. Rest in peace, Bennie, you will never be forgotten.

Afterword

A True Champion of Life

By Cynthia Biggs El

A **sucker punch** is argot or slang for an unexpected blow that comes suddenly and without warning. It allows no time on the part of the intended for preparation in defense, often resulting in major damage.

In the sport of boxing, the term is generally reserved for that moment when delivery of such a punch is deemed unethical, culpable, and in violation of the rules of the fight game. Outside of the ring it is sometimes referenced as a random assault.

Consequently, from either perspective, one might raise the question, “What could possibly be ‘sweet’ about a sucker punch?”

In life we all are subject to devastating blows, ominous sudden turns, and dire disappointments. At times such staggering effects will seem to be riding roughshod over us – when the very thought of what we are experiencing is enough to render even the strongest among us punch drunk. In this compromised and vulnerable state, problems seemingly loom as insurmountable, as we go down for the count, stunned by the rapid flurry of life's pressures.

However, as so artfully portrayed between each line of Xavier's heart-warming autobiographical narratives, during any face off with what may appear to be inevitable defeat, your comeback is vested in the mettle you execute in confronting life's most fierce opponents.

What is "sweet" about a sucker punch is the resulting essence that culminates from the ability to call up *unbeatable will* when least expected to return power shot after power shot, overthrowing unmitigated adversity with every strike.

This book is a proven testament that you can combat hardship, negativity, and any obstacles that come your way with your own left-right combinations of love, truth, peace, freedom, and justice, and re-surface as the victor – come out on top. This is the stuff of the vindicator, the blazon of honor of a true Champion of Life, for in the words of Sheik Sharif Abdul Ali, "Without a foe, a soldier never knows his strength."

About the Author

An ex-professional boxer from Philadelphia's highly cultured fight scene, Xavier Biggs pursued a career in boxing to rehabilitate his life from the effects of growing up on the hard streets of Philly. He met with major frustration after turning down a contract proposal from a local promoter, which actually turned out to be a great learning experience that helped qualify him to accompany his younger brother “Tyrell” in his quest to capture the world heavyweight championship title after winning the gold medal in the first ever super heavyweight division in the 1984 Olympic Games in Los Angeles.

While Xavier was in the training camp, his mind was like a sponge soaking up every drop of boxing knowledge he could absorb from the experts. He also savored associations and experiences with world champions and world-class boxers of this era. Xavier eventually moved to Atlanta and utilized his acquired business acumen to open 5 boxing gyms, pioneered a successful boxing fitness program, and helped several amateur and professional fighters, some of which went on to become division champions.

Currently, Xavier is training yet another iconic

figure, Grammy-award winning recording artist, dancer, and actor, Usher, who is preparing to play boxing great Sugar Ray Leonard in the upcoming movie production *Hands of Stone*, the story of Roberto Duran.

Usher not only made the cover, but is featured in the November 2013 25th Anniversary issue of Men's Health Magazine, which also showcases one of Xavier's sample workouts for the recording artist turned film star boxer in training.

Made in the USA
Charleston, SC
23 September 2014